Basics

conditioning thread

Conditioning straightens and strengthens your thread and also helps it resist fraying, separating, and tangling. Pull unwaxed nylon threads like Nymo through either beeswax (not candle wax or paraffin) or Thread Heaven to condition. Beeswax adds tackiness that is useful if you want your beadwork to fit tightly. Thread Heaven adds a static charge that causes the thread to repel itself, so it can't be used with doubled thread. All nylon threads stretch, so maintain tension on the thread as you condition it.

flattened crimp

1 Hold the crimp bead using the tip of your chainnose pliers. Squeeze the pliers firmly to flatten the crimp. Tug the clasp to make sure the crimp has a solid grip on the wire. If the wire slides, remove the crimp bead and repeat the steps with a new crimp bead.
2 Test that the flattened crimp is secure.

folded crimp

1 Position the crimp bead in the notch closest to the crimping pliers' handle.
2 Separate the wires and firmly squeeze the crimp.

3 Move the crimp into the notch at the pliers' tip and hold the crimp as shown.

Squeeze the crimp bead, folding it in half at the indentation.
4 Test that the flattened crimp is secure.

plain loop

1 Trim the wire ⅜ in. (1cm) above the top bead. Make a right angle bend close to the bead.
2 Grab the wire's tip with roundnose pliers. Roll the wire to form a half circle. Release the wire.

3 Reposition the pliers in the loop and continue rolling.
4 The finished loop should form a centered circle above the bead.

wrapped loop

1 Make sure you have at least 1¼ in. (3.2cm) of wire above the bead. With the tip of your chainnose pliers, grasp the wire directly above the bead. Bend the wire (above the pliers) into a right angle.
2 Using roundnose pliers, position the jaws vertically in the bend.

3 Bring the wire over the top jaw of the roundnose pliers.
4 Keep the jaws vertical and reposition

t̲
loop. Curve the wire a̲...̲ the bottom of the roundnose pliers. This is the first half of a wrapped loop.
5 Position the chainnose pliers' jaws across the loop.
6 Wrap the wire around the wire stem, covering the stem between the loop and the top bead. Trim the excess wire and press the cut end close to the wraps with chainnose pliers.

jump rings

1 Hold the jump ring with two pairs of chainnose pliers or chainnose and roundnose pliers, as shown.
2 To open the jump ring, bring one pair of pliers toward you and push the other pair away.

3 Reverse the steps to close the open jump ring.

surgeon's knot

Cross the right end over the left and go through loop. Go through loop again. Pull ends to tighten. Cross the left end over the right and go through once. Pull the ends to tighten.

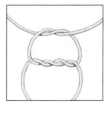

Basics

half-hitch knot

Come out a bead and form a loop perpendicular to the thread between beads. Bring the needle under the thread away from the loop. Then go back over the thread and through the loop. Pull gently so the knot doesn't tighten prematurely.

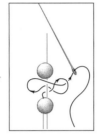

peyote: flat even-count

1 String one bead and loop through it again in the same direction (remove the extra loop and weave the tail into the work after a few rows). String beads to total an even number. In peyote stitch, rows are nestled together and counted diagonally, so these beads actually comprise the first two rows.

2 To begin row 3 (the numbers in the drawings below indicate rows), pick up a bead and stitch through the second bead from the end. Pick up a bead and go through the fourth bead from the end. Continue in this manner. End by going through the first bead strung.

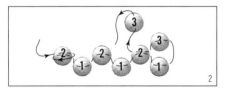

3 To start row 4 and all other rows, pick up a bead and go through the last bead added on the previous row.

To end a thread, weave through the work in a zigzag path, tying two half-hitch knots (see instructions at left) along the way. Go through a few more beads before trimming the thread close to the work.

To resume stitching, anchor a new thread in the work with half-hitch knots, zigzag through the work, and exit the last bead added in the same direction. Continue stitching where you left off.

peyote: circular even-count

1 String an even number of beads to equal the desired circumference. Tie in a circle, leaving some ease.
2 Even-numbered beads form row 1 and odd-numbered beads, row 2. (Numbers indicate rows.) Put the ring over a form if desired. Go through the first bead to the left of the knot. Pick up a bead (#1 of row 3), skip a bead, and go through the next bead. Repeat around until you're back to the start.

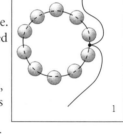

3 Since you started with an even number of beads, you need to work a step up to be in position for the next row. Go through the first beads on rows 2 and 3. Pick up a bead and go through the second bead of row 3; continue. (If you begin with an odd number of beads, there won't be a step up; you'll keep spiraling.)

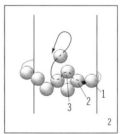

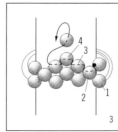

join peyote pieces

To join two sections of a flat peyote piece invisibly, match up the two pieces so the edge beads fit together. "Zip up" the pieces by zigzagging through each edge bead.

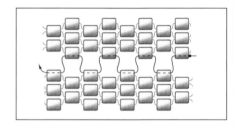

ladder and brick stitch

1 A ladder of seed or bugle beads is most often used to begin brick stitch: Pick up two beads. Leave a 3-4-in. (.08-.1m) tail

and go through both beads again in the same direction. Pull the top bead down so the beads are side by side. The thread exits the bottom of bead #2. String bead #3 and go back through #2 from top to bottom. Come back up #3.

String bead #4. Go through #3 from bottom to top and #4 from top to bottom. Add odd-numbered beads like #3 and even-numbered beads like #4.

To stabilize the ladder, zigzag back through all the beads.
2 To begin each row so no thread shows on the edge, string two beads. Go under the thread between the second and third beads on the ladder from back to front. Pull tight. Go up the second bead added, then down the first. Come back up the second bead.
3 For the remaining stitches on each row, pick up one bead. Go under the next loop on the row below from back to front. Go back up the new bead.

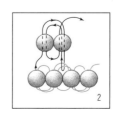

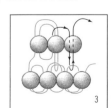

Peyote bead bracelet

These small peyote-stitched cylinders are easy and quick and make a stunning bracelet. The small cylinders are self-supporting so no additional beads or forms are necessary.

The beads are made with flat, even-count peyote stitch—the easiest peyote technique of all—and are then spaced out with small silver, gold-plated, crystal, or matte glass beads. If you're new to peyote stitch, after your second or third bead, you'll feel like a pro. Best of all, in only a few hours, you'll have a beautiful bracelet and a new skill to show off.

making a peyote bead

❶ Thread the needle with about 24 in. (61cm) of Nymo D beading thread and make a flat piece of peyote six beads wide and ten rows long (see "Basics," p. 3).

❷ When finished, the flat edges will each be five beads long. Now join the two saw-toothed edges together by zigzagging through the high beads (see "Basics" and **photo a**).

❸ Weave each tail diagonally into the beadwork and tie a half-hitch knot (see "Basics") between beads. Repeat. Go through two or three more beads and clip the thread close to the work.

determining length

❶ If you have a small wrist, make 12 peyote beads and use 13 of the faceted silver beads (to start and end and go between peyote beads). The bracelet will be 7¼ in. (18cm) long.

❷ For an average to slightly larger than average wrist, make 13 peyote beads and use 12 faceted beads between them. The bracelet will be 7¾ in. (20cm) long.

stringing the bracelet

❶ String a crimp bead and then the soldered ring onto the flexible beading wire. Bring the short end of wire back through the crimp. Crimp the crimp bead (see "Basics").

❷ For a short bracelet (7¼ in.), string a faceted bead, bringing the short tail through it and then trimming the tail with wire cutters. Then string a 2mm bead. Now string a peyote bead, a 2mm bead, a faceted bead, and a 2mm bead. Add ten more of these sets, ending with a peyote bead, a 2mm bead, and a faceted bead.

For a long bracelet (7¾ in.), the set consists of a peyote bead, a 2mm bead, a faceted bead, and a 2mm bead. String 12 sets. Then end with a peyote bead.

❸ String the second crimp and then the clasp and go back through the crimp and the last bead (**photo b**). Tighten the beading wire, but not so much that the bracelet is stiff. Crimp the crimp bead. ❍

– *Sue Jackson and Wendy Hubick*

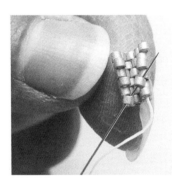

a

b

materials

- 22g Delica beads, here 22k gold-plated matte finish
- **13** 4mm faceted sterling silver beads
- **24** 2mm sterling silver beads
- 3 x 9mm sterling silver lobster clasp
- 3mm soldered sterling silver jump ring
- 10 in. (25cm) flexible beading wire, .014
- beading needles, #10 or 12
- Nymo D beading thread
- beeswax or Thread Heaven for Nymo

Tools: wire cutters, chainnose or crimping pliers

Peyote tube bead necklace

Learn to read a peyote-stitch graph as you make these colorful beaded beads, reminiscent of a geometric mosaic.

Work each graph in even-count, flat peyote stitch. After completing the main section of each graph, add the beads in the far-right column using brick stitch. It's much easier to work in even-count peyote and add a brick-stitch row along the finished edge than to work in odd-count peyote for the entire piece.

The easiest way to read a graph is to use a row marker, such as a ruler, to help you keep track of the rows as you stitch. You can start either at the top row and work down the chart or at the bottom and work up. If you follow these instructions, you'll be starting at the top left edge of each graph.

beaded beads

❶ Thread a needle with 2 yd. (1.8m) of waxed Nymo. String a bead to use as a stop bead and slide it about 6 in. (15cm) from the tail end. Go through the stop bead again in the same direction. Don't count this bead as part of the design; you'll remove it later.

❷ Start reading the chart from the upper left-hand corner and begin the pattern in **figure 1** by picking up beads for the first two peyote rows, as follows: one aqua, two purple, three blue, three purple, three blue, three purple, three blue, two purple. All subsequent rows are worked one at a time.

❸ Start row 3 by reading the graph from right to left. Work in flat peyote (see "Basics," p. 3) across the row.

❹ Work row 4 from left to right. Continue to follow the graph, keeping track of the rows with your marker. Compare your beadwork to the charted pattern frequently to make sure your work is correct. If you lose track of your place, turn your work so the stop bead and thread tails are at the corner at upper left.

❺ When you've finished the peyote portion of this bead, your thread should be

start

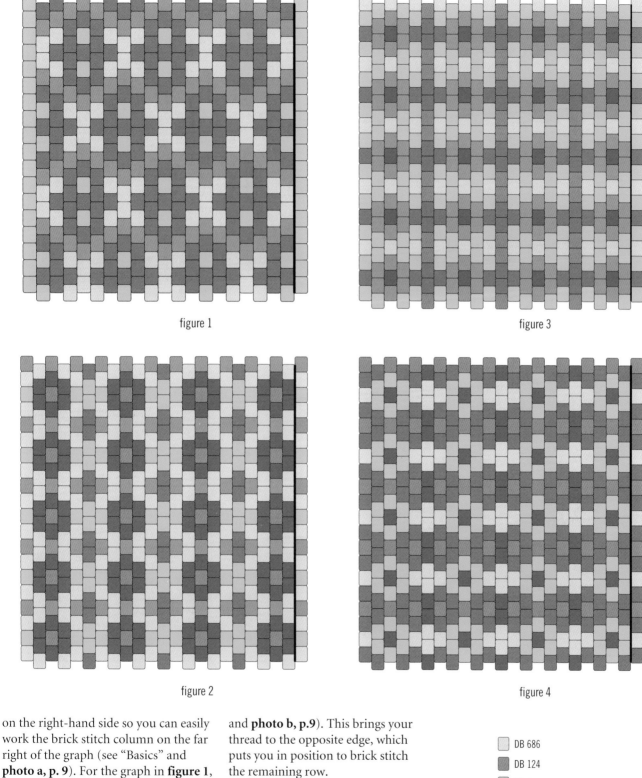

figure 1

figure 3

figure 2

figure 4

on the right-hand side so you can easily work the brick stitch column on the far right of the graph (see "Basics" and **photo a, p. 9**). For the graph in **figure 1**, brick stitch a row using silver-lined aqua beads.

If you find that your thread is on the wrong edge to work the brick stitch row, form the cylinder first. Line up the top and bottom of the beadwork and zip up the two edges (see "Basics"

and **photo b, p.9**). This brings your thread to the opposite edge, which puts you in position to brick stitch the remaining row.

❻ If you haven't yet zipped up the two edges, sew the cylinder together as described above.

❼ Secure the thread in the beadwork with half-hitch knots (see "Basics"). Remove the stop bead, thread a needle on the tail end, and secure the thread

☐	DB 686
☐	DB 124
☐	DB 044
☐	DB 177
☐	DB 183
☐	DB 923

as before. Trim the thread close to the beadwork.

❽ Make a second bead following the chart in **figure 1**. Make one bead using the chart in **figure 2** and two beads each using the charts in **figures 3** and **4**.

stringing the necklace

❶ Determine the finished length of your necklace, add 4 in. (10cm), and cut a piece of flexible beading wire to that length.

❷ String a crimp bead and half the clasp on the beading wire. Go back through the crimp bead, leaving a 2-in. (5cm) tail. Keep the wire slightly loose around the clasp. Crimp the crimp bead (see "Basics") and trim the wire tail to ¼ in. (6mm).

❸ String about 2 in. of accent beads, or the length you desire, before stringing the first beaded bead. Make sure the accent beads cover the short wire tail.

❹ String one disk-shaped bead and about 1⅛ in. (3cm) of filler beads onto the beading wire. (Keep the length of filler beads slightly shorter than the beaded beads.) Slide a cylinder gently over the filler beads (**photo c**). If the fit is tight, work slowly to give the thread a chance to stretch, and be careful not to break the cylinders. The small space remaining on each side of the filler allows the disk-shaped beads to sit slightly inside the beaded bead. String another disk-shaped bead to finish the beaded bead's open end.

Use moderately heavy beads as filler to help the necklace hang well. Don't use heavy beads, however, if your necklace is long enough to hit something when it swings. The weight might cause the cylinder beads to break.

❺ Continue stringing accent beads,

a

charms, and beaded beads, as desired. If you incorporate lampworked beads, as shown here, you may need to fill their holes with smaller beads. Use leftover cylinders or small seed beads to fill the large holes, so the lampwork beads will hang nicely on your necklace.

❻ When you're done stringing the necklace, pick up a crimp bead and the remaining clasp half. Finish as in step 2, above, tucking the wire tail into the end beads. ❍ – *Linda Richmond*

Sparkling beaded beads

Beaded beads are often made as individual elements. But in this clever design, the beaded beads are made while you string your necklace. Each one consists of a bugle bead that is wrapped by five rows of fire-polished beads and seed beads, or whatever beads appeal to you. This versatile design looks good many ways.

Because bugle beads have sharp edges, smooth their ends with an emery board before stringing them, and use resilient Fireline thread to prevent breakage.

aqua necklace

❶ Start with 2½ yd. (2.3m) of Fireline. String a size 11º seed bead, go back through it in the same direction, and tie the two ends together with a surgeon's knot (see "Basics," p. 3). Go back through the bead again and glue the knot. After the glue dries, trim the tail to ⅛ in. (3mm) and string a bead tip from the hook end. Close the bead tip over the bead.

❷ String an alternating pattern of one size 8º seed bead and one 3mm fire-polished (FP) bead until you have seven beads. String a size 2 bugle.

❸ String a size 11º seed bead, a 3mm FP bead, and an 11º seed bead. Tighten to remove any slack along the strand and sew back through the bugle in the same direction (**photo a**).

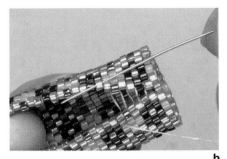

b

c

Kits for these beaded beads are available. Call (208) 265-7917 or see Linda's website, www.lindarichmond.com.

materials

- Japanese cylinder beads (Delicas) in each of the following quantities and colors:
  - 6g DB 923 purple
  - 5g DB 044 aqua
  - 4g DB 686 chartreuse
  - 4g DB 177 blue
  - 2g DB 124 sage
  - 2g DB 183 dark blue
- 2½ in. (6.4cm) of 8mm beads (to fill small beaded beads—figure 1)
- 6 in. (15cm) of 10mm beads (to fill large beaded beads)
- **14** 12mm disk-shaped beads (these are by Paula Radke)

- assorted beads to complement beaded beads
- charms (those shoewn here are by Ashes to Beauty Adornments)
- flexible beading wire, .014
- Nymo B beading thread
- beeswax or Thread Heaven
- beading needles, #12
- **2** crimp beads
- clasp (the onme shown here is by Ashes to Beauty Adornments)

Tools: chainnose or crimping pliers, wire cutters

---

④ Repeat step 3 four times, enclosing the bugle bead in five rows of beads.

⑤ Repeat steps 2-4 eight times.

⑥ String an alternating pattern of one size 8º seed bead and one 3mm FP bead until you have seven beads. String a 6mm FP, a 3mm FP, a faceted crystal rondelle, a 3mm FP, and a size 5 bugle.

⑦ String an 11º, a 3mm FP, a 4mm FP, a 3mm FP, and an 11º. Sew back through the bugle bead. Repeat four times to surround the bugle with five rows (**photo b**).

⑧ Finish the other side of the necklace with nine beaded beads to match the first side.

⑨ String a bead tip and a size 11º seed bead. Sew back through the bead tip and two beads. Tie a half-hitch knot, go through a few more beads, and tie another half-hitch knot (see "Basics"). Glue the knots, go through a few more beads, and trim the tail.

⑩ Curve the hook of each bead tip around a jump ring with roundnose pliers. Attach each ring to one clasp half.

purple necklace

❶ Repeat step 1 above.

❷ String a repeating pattern of one size 8º seed bead and one 3mm blue iris FP beads for a total of five beads. String a size 2 bugle.

❸ Repeat steps 3-4 of "aqua necklace," using 3mm lavender FP beads.

❹ Repeat steps 2-3 eight times to make a total of nine wrapped beads in the following order: two lavender, one blue iris, one lavender, one blue iris, one lavender, three blue iris.

❺ String a repeating pattern of one size 8º seed bead and one 3mm FP for a total of five beads. String a 4mm FP bead, a 5mm accent bead, a 4mm FP bead, and a size 4 bugle.

❻ String a 3mm lavender FP, a 4mm blue iris FP, and a 3mm lavender FP. Sew back through the bugle bead. Repeat

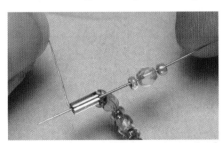

a

b

four more times to surround the bugle.

❼ Follow steps 8-10 of "aqua necklace" to complete the project. ❍

– Linda Gettings

materials

aqua necklace

- **164** 3mm faceted fire-polished beads, aqua
- **5** 4mm faceted FP beads, aqua
- **2** 6mm faceted FP beads, aqua
- **2** 8mm faceted crystal rondelles, clear
- **10g** size 8º seed beads, silver-lined aqua
- **10g** size 11º seed beads, aqua
- **18** size 2 (5mm) bugle beads, silver
- size 5 (12mm) bugle bead, silver

purple necklace

- **86** 3mm faceted FP beads, blue iris
- **40** 3mm faceted FP beads, lavender
- **9** 4mm faceted FP beads, blue iris
- **2** 5mm accent beads
- **10g** size 8º seed beads, lavender
- **10g** size 11º seed beads, blue iris
- **18** size 2 (5mm) bugle beads, purple
- size 4 (10mm) bugle bead, purple

both necklaces

- Fireline fishing line, 6-lb. test
- beading needles, #12
- **2** bead tips per necklace
- **2** jump rings per necklace
- clasp, magnetic or toggle
- G-S Hypo Cement

Tools: chainnose and roundnose pliers

Right-angle-weave beaded bead

Single-needle right-angle weave is a flexible stitch that drapes beautifully. Each stitch is worked with a group of four or more beads that form a square. If you use more than four beads per stitch, each side of the square has the same number of beads and the center is open. In the case of this bead, you don't want the base bead to show, so the four-bead version of the stitch works best. Increasing and decreasing are easy in right-angle weave, but it's even easier to cover a bead by decreasing the size of the beads used as you approach the hole. In this case, you only have to make two or three decrease stitches in the very last row.

A single beaded bead strung on beaded memory wire makes a strong statement. Alternatively, you could make as many beaded beads as you wish for your necklace. If you use different sizes of wooden core beads, experiment with the number of stitches and the size of beads you need to cover the core bead most effectively.

starting

❶ If desired, paint the wooden bead and let it dry.

❷ Thread a needle with about 2 yd. (1.8m) of Nymo. Make a chain of right-angle-weave stitches using the largest beads, the rondelles, as follows:

To start the first row, string four beads and tie into a snug circle. Pass the needle through the first three beads again (**figure 1**).

Pick up three beads and sew back through the end bead of the previous circle and the first two new beads (**figure 2**).

Pick up three beads and sew back through the end bead of the previous circle and the first two new beads

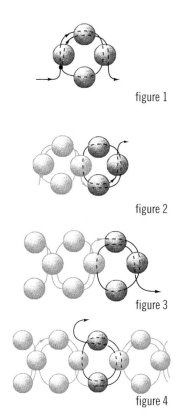

figure 1

figure 2

figure 3

figure 4

a

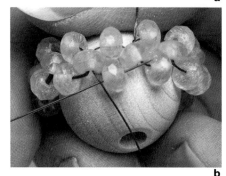

b

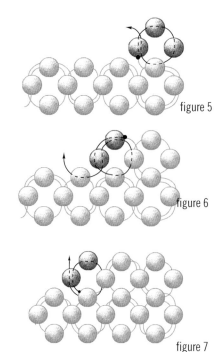

figure 5

figure 6

figure 7

figure 8

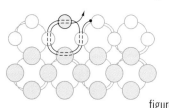

c

d

(**figure 3**). Continue adding three beads for each stitch until the first row is the desired length. You are sewing circles in a figure-8 pattern and alternating direction with each stitch.

❸ Join the chain into a ring with a final stitch as shown in **figure 4**: With the needle exiting the end bead of the line of stitches, string one bead. Making sure the chain is not twisted, bring the first stitch around to meet the last, forming a circle. Go through the end bead of the first stitch. String one bead and go through the end bead of the last stitch.

❹ Make sure the ring of stitches fits around the middle of the wooden bead (**photo a**). Then go through beads of the final stitch for security, exiting an edge bead (**photo b**).

beading the bead
You can work the first half of the beaded cover for the wooden bead on the large bead or not, as you prefer.

❶ Work the second row of right-angle weave with size 6º seed beads as follows:

Exiting an edge bead on row 1, pick up three beads and sew back through the bead you just exited and the first new bead (**figure 5**).

materials
- 20mm wooden bead
- **120** size 11º seed beads
- **50** size 8º seed beads
- **200** size 6º seed beads
- **44** 5 x 3.2mm pressed glass rondelles
- 18½ in. (47cm) necklace memory wire
- Nymo D beading thread
- beeswax or Thread Heaven
- beading needles, #12

Tools: chainnose and roundnose pliers
Optional: clasp and 2 split rings, acrylic paint to match or contrast with the main bead color

Pick up two beads and sew through the next top bead of the row below and the last bead of the previous stitch. Continue through the new beads and the next top bead on the row below (**figure 6**).

Keep stitching in a figure-8; don't sew straight lines between stitches. Pick up two beads for each of the remaining stitches on the row, alternating directions as shown in **figures 6** and **7**.

❷ To work the final stitch and join the row into a circle, go through the end bead of the last stitch, the edge bead on the row below, and the end bead of the first stitch (**photo c**). String one bead and repeat this thread path, exiting the top bead (**figure 8**).

❸ Work one row of size 8º seed beads

off the top beads of the size 6º row as in step 1-2 of "beading the bead."

❹ Work one row of size 11º seed beads off the top beads of the size 8º row as in steps 1-2 of "beading the bead."

❺ Put the beadwork on the wooden bead with the rondelle row around the

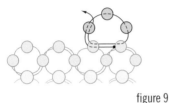

figure 9

e

f

g

circumference (**photo d**). The last row of size 11º seed beads will require three to six decrease stitches to fit snugly around the hole. Try to space the decreases evenly.

❻ Start with a decrease. With your needle exiting the top bead on the last row, continue through the next top bead, pick up three beads and go through the two top beads and the first added bead (**figure 9** and **photo e**).

❼ Work a normal stitch. When the next two top beads seem jammed together, work another decrease. Continue in this manner until you have joined the first and last stitch of the decrease row.

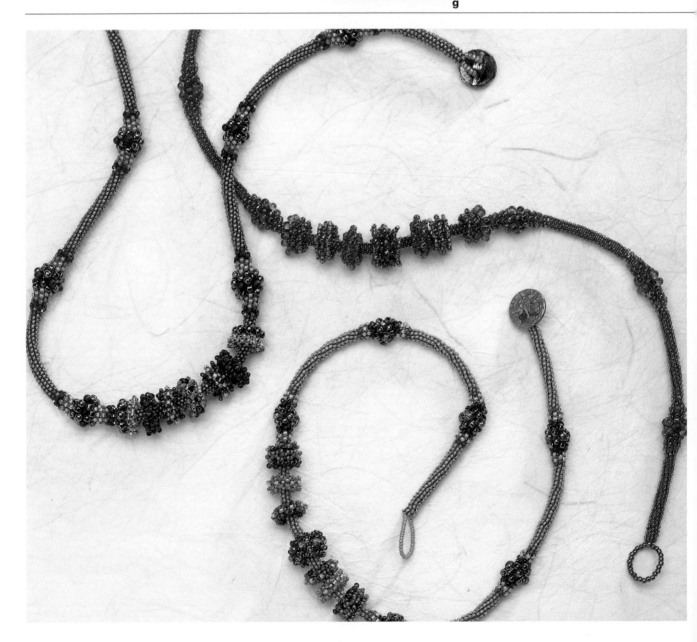

If you're using Japanese size 11º seed beads rather than Czech beads, you'll have to decrease more frequently because Japanese 11ºs are larger than Czech 11ºs. Pick the thinnest beads for this row.

8 With your needle exiting a top bead, go through all the top beads on the final row to pull them together into a neat ring around the bead's hole (**photo f**). Repeat the thread path to reinforce the ring.

9 Follow the thread path of the right-angle-weave stitches to exit a bead on the other side of the long edge of the rondelle row (**photo g**).

10 With the beadwork on the wooden bead, repeat steps 1-8 of "beading the bead" on the second half of the bead.

11 Weave both tails into the beadwork tying two or three half-hitch knots (see "Basics," p. 3) between beads. Go through a few more beads and trim the tail close to the work.

making a necklace

1 Turn the bead cover so the rings of 11ºs are over each of the holes and thread the bead to the center of an 18½-in. (47cm) length of necklace memory wire.

2 To make the necklace as shown on page 10, string three size 6ºs. Then repeat this pattern four times: string an 8º or 11º, a rondelle, an 8º or 11º, and nine or ten size 6ºs. End with an 8º or 11º, a rondelle, an 8º or 11º, and 21-24 size 6ºs.

3 Use roundnose pliers to turn a loop in the last ⅜-½ in. (1-1.3cm) of the memory wire (see steps 2-3 of "making loops" in "Basics"). When turning a loop in memory wire do not bend the wire at a right angle first because it will break.

4 Repeat steps 2-3 of "making a necklace" on the other side of the bead.

5 If you wish, attach a clasp to the back loops with split rings. ●
– Alice Korach

Floating rings necklace

Most beaded beads are strung on cord, wire, or thread just like ordinary beads. Here, however, the beads are made with large centers so they can be strung on a peyote rope. The beaded rings are captured in the center of the necklace, and the surprise is that they can spin and slide around.

This necklace has seven beaded beads. There are three pairs and one centerpiece bead. Make as few as three or as many as nine beads, and feel free to make each different. If you want to add more than nine beads, make more rows in the center section of your rope so all the beads fit.

beaded beads

1 Thread a needle with 1 yd. (.9m) of Nymo or Fireline. String 18 size 11º seed beads. Tie the beads into a circle with a surgeon's knot (see "Basics," p. 3), leaving a 5-in. (13cm) tail. There should be some ease between the beads.

2 Sew through the bead next to the knot. String an 11º, skip a bead, and go through the next bead (**photo a**). Continue working in even-count tubular peyote (see "Basics") for a total of five rows.

3 String three 15º seeds and go through the next edge bead (**photo b**). Repeat around the outside of the peyote ring. When you add the last set of 15ºs, bring the needle through the first 11º and the one diagonally below it to the left (**photo c**). Go through one more bead diagonally below so your needle exits a bead on the third row of the ring.

4 String a 15º, an 11º, and a 15º and go through the next bead in the row (**photo d, p. 14**). Repeat around the center of the ring. On the last set, bring the needle through the 11º and diagonally through the 11ºs below until the needle exits an edge bead on the unembellished side (**photo e, p. 14**).

5 Add three 15ºs between every edge bead as in step 3 (**photo f, p. 14**).

6 End the thread by tying two or three half-hitch knots (see "Basics") between beads. Trim it. Repeat with the tail.

7 Repeat steps 1-6 to make a second bead to match the first.

8 Make two more two-bead sets using different color combinations. Also try starting the embellishment on the second row of the ring, or add embellishment to each row. You can also vary the number of rows in each ring. For one set of beads, for instance,

a

b

c

make a ring with three rows and on the last row string a tiny teardrop between each edge bead. This is the fun part—experiment!

9 For the center bead, make a ring with five rows and embellish the center row with a 15º, a 3mm fire-polished bead, and a 15º between each bead. Embellish the edges of the ring.

peyote rope

This pattern is for a necklace 17½-in. (45cm) long, not including the clasp.

1 Thread a needle with a 2-yd. (1.8m) length of Nymo or Fireline. String eight 15º main color (MC) seed beads. Tie the beads into a circle with a surgeon's knot, leaving an 8-in. (20cm) tail.

2 Work in tubular peyote for a total of 40 rows.

3 Pick up the accent color (AC) 15ºs for the next three rows.

Use size 11º seeds for three rows (**photo g**).

Keeping the tension firm so the thread doesn't show, work two rows with 8º seeds (**photo h**).

4 Work the next row with your accent beads (**photo i**).

5 Reverse the rows in step 3, stitching eight more rows with the last three rows being 15ºs.

6 Repeat steps 2-5 twice more.

7 Now you are at the middle section of the necklace. Using 15º MC seeds, work 95 rows of tubular peyote. If you are adding more beaded beads, you might need to add a few extra rows to this section so the beads can move freely.

d

e

f

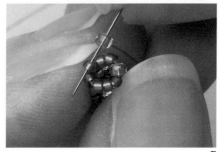

g

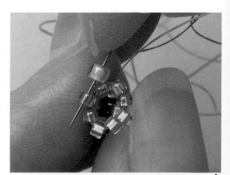

h

i

j

k

materials

- 15g size 15º Japanese seed beads, main color
- 2g size 15º Japanese seed beads, each of one or two colors
- 2g size 11º Japanese seed beads, each of one to three colors
- 3g size 8º seed beads
- assorted accent beads: teardrops, 3-4mm crystals, size 6º seed beads, etc.
- button or bead for the clasp
- Nymo B beading thread or Fireline fishing line, 6-lb. test
- beeswax or Thread Heaven for Nymo
- beading needles, #12

8 String the beaded beads on the peyote rope.

9 Make the second half of the necklace to match the first. You will have three accent bead sections on each side of the sliding rings.

10 Bring the needle and thread through the four edge beads on the last row to close the end of the peyote tube.

11 String five 15ºs, go through the loop on the button, string five 15ºs, and go through a bead on the other side of the peyote rope (**photo j**). Retrace the thread path (**photo k**) a couple of times for stability and

end the thread with half-hitch knots.

12 Thread a needle on the tail at the other end and repeat step 10. String enough 15ºs to make a loop that fits around the button. Reinforce the loop with several thread passes and end the thread. ❍ – *Bonnie O'Donnell-Painter*

Prickly beads

Adding spikes to a beaded bead not only customizes your jewelry but also adds wonderful textural interest. Each bead takes about an hour to make at first. But once you get the pattern down, you will be able to make them much faster.

The wrapped loops on each of these beaded beads have double loops. You may use regular wrapped loops (see "Basics," p. 3) instead if you prefer.

getting started

❶ Cut a 5-in. (13cm) piece of 22-gauge wire. Make the first half of a wrapped loop (see "Basics") about 2 in. (5cm) from one end of the wire.

❷ Reposition the pliers and make a second loop next to the first by wrapping the short wire around one jaw of the pliers until it touches the other jaw (**photo a, p. 16**). Reposition the pliers again and complete the loop—stop when the wire is perpendicular to the long wire (under both loops). Complete the wrapped loops (see "Basics") and trim the tail.

❸ String an 8mm bead (that you will bead over) against the wrap. Leave about ⅛-in. (3mm) of space after the bead and make a wrapped double loop in the same plane as the first (**photo b, p. 16**).

❹ Repeat steps 1-3 with all the 8mm beads you will bead over.

beaded base

If you are using Nymo, condition it with beeswax. A fair amount of tension (not too tight and not too loose—you will get the feel for it as you work) simplifies this beading process. Once you find the right tension, the beads will line up nicely, and you will find it easier to see where the next bead needs to be added. The base is worked using only the main color 11°s. Check off the rows as you go so you don't get confused. It is difficult to count the rows and find your place if you have to stop.

❶ Thread a beading needle with a 1½-yd. (1.4m) length of Nymo.

Row 1: String eight 11° seed beads 6 in. (15cm) from the end of the thread. Go through the beads again in the same direction to form a ring. Place the ring over the double loop on the bead (**photo c, p. 16**). Pull the ring of beads snug against each other and tie the tail and the working thread together with a surgeon's knot (see "Basics").

Row 2: Bring the needle through the first bead, string a bead, and go through the next two beads in the ring (**figure 1, a-b**). Repeat around the ring until the thread exits the first bead in row 2 (**figure 1, b-c**).

Row 3: String three beads and go through the next bead on the second row (**figure 2, a-b**). Repeat around the ring adding three beads between each bead added in row 2 (**figure 2, b-c**). Go through the first three-bead set (**figure 2, c-d**) so the needle is in position to start the next row.

Row 4: String one bead and go through a three-bead set (**figure 3, a-b**). Repeat until the thread exits the first bead added in the row (**figure 3, c-d**).

Row 5: String one bead and go through the middle bead of the three-bead set from row 3 (**figure 4, a-b**). String a bead and go through the bead sticking up (the bead added on row 4) (**figure 4, b-c**). Repeat until the thread exits the first bead added (**figure 4, c-d**).

Row 6: String two beads, go through the bead sticking up (**figure 5, a-b**). String one bead and go through the next "up" bead (**figure 5, b-c**). Repeat until the thread exits the first two beads added (**figure 5, c-d**).

You are now at the center of the bead and the remaining rows will decrease until you are back to an eight-bead ring.

Row 7: String one bead, go through the up bead (**figure 6, a-b**). String one bead and go through the two up beads (**figure 6, b-c**). Repeat until the thread exits the first bead added (**figure 6, c-d**).

Row 8: String one bead and go through the next up bead. Repeat until the thread exits the first bead (adding eight beads total).

Row 9: Repeat row 8.

Row 10: Go through the next up bead (decrease without adding a bead), string one bead, and go through the next up bead. Repeat (adding four beads total) until the thread exits the first bead added (**photo d**).

Row 11: String two beads and go through the up bead. Repeat. This is the last row and will be a ring of eight beads. Both ends of the bead will look the same (**photo e**).

❷ The rest of the bead is worked with

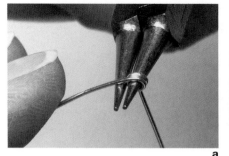

a

c

b

d

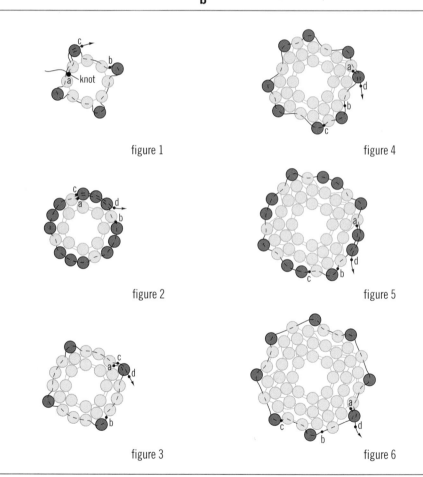

figure 1

figure 4

figure 2

figure 5

figure 3

figure 6

doubled thread. Reposition the needle on the thread so the tail extends past the beaded bead. Retrace the thread path of the ring (row 11) with the doubled thread (**photo f**). The thread will exit a two-bead set. Trim the tail, not the doubled working thread. The

finished base will look like **photo g**.

❸ Repeat steps 1-2 with the other 8mm base beads.

spike embellishment

❶ Tight tension is needed so each spike embellishment stands up.

e

g

i

f

h

j

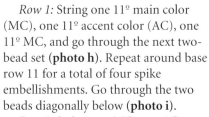

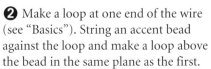

Row 1: String one 11º main color (MC), one 11º accent color (AC), one 11º MC, and go through the next two-bead set (**photo h**). Repeat around base row 11 for a total of four spike embellishments. Go through the two beads diagonally below (**photo i**).

Row 2: String one MC, one AC, one MC, and go through the next bead in the base row. Repeat for a total of eight spikes. Go through the three beads diagonally below.

Row 3: The thread now exits a bead in base row 6 (the middle row), where the beads alternate 2 and 1. String an 8º seed and one MC. Go back through the 8º and the next bead(s) in the base row (**photo j**). Repeat for a total of eight spikes. Go through three beads diagonally below.

Row 4: Repeat row 2 and then position the needle so it exits a two-bead set on base row 1.

Row 5: Repeat row 1 to add four more spikes.

❷ Weave the thread through a few beads of the base and tie a few half-hitch knots (see "Basics") between base beads. Trim the excess thread. Repeat with the starting tail.

❸ Repeat steps 1-2 with the remaining base beads.

accent bead links

❶ Cut a piece of 16- or 18-gauge wire 1 in. (2.5cm) longer than the glass accent bead.

❷ Make a loop at one end of the wire (see "Basics"). String an accent bead against the loop and make a loop above the bead in the same plane as the first.

❸ Repeat steps 1-2 with the remaining accent beads.

necklace assembly

❶ Open a 5mm jump ring sideways (see "Basics") and slide it through a loop on an accent bead and a double loop on a beaded bead. Close the loop.

❷ Continue connecting an alternating pattern of accent beads and beaded beads with jump rings until you reach the desired length. So the necklace hangs comfortably on your neck, link two or three accent beads at each end before you attach the clasp (use 6mm beads if your main accent beads are 9-14mm).

❸ Attach the clasp with a jump ring or open a loop on the last bead and slide it through the loop on the clasp. Repeat with the other side.

crystal dangles (optional)

❶ String a crystal on a head pin and make a loop. Repeat with the remaining crystals.

❷ Use a 4mm jump ring to attach each dangle to a 5mm jump ring between an accent and a beaded bead. Each 5mm jump ring has two crystal dangles. ◉
– *Rachel Nelson*

materials

- 40g size 11º Japanese seed beads (main color—MC)
- 20g size 11º Japanese seed beads (accent color—AC)
- 10g size 6º or 8º seed beads
- **8-10** 8mm glass beads (to bead over)
- **8** 9-12mm or **14** 8mm accent glass beads
- **4-6** 6mm accent glass beads (if using 9-12mm beads above)
- 4 ft. (1.2m) 22-gauge sterling silver wire, half hard
- 2-3 ft. (61-91cm) 16- or 18-gauge sterling silver wire, half hard
- **22-26** 5mm 18-gauge jump rings
- lobster claw or hook clasp with a jump or split ring
- Nymo B beading thread or Fireline fishing line, 6-lb. test
- beeswax for Nymo
- beading needles, #12

Tools: roundnose and chainnose pliers, diagonal wire cutters

Optional: 36 4mm Austrian crystals, **36** head pins, **36** 4mm jump rings

A new twist on beads

a

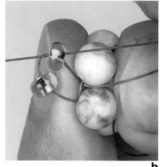

b

c

d

This booklet shows several ways to make beaded beads, including some hollow ones. But this one is a little different— it's a large self-supporting bead that involves two stitches. This technique works with many different kinds of beads.

Weave the foundation of the bead in tubular brick stitch using decreasing bead sizes. Then create tension and shape the bead by working caddis weave in the opposite direction. You can try this technique with a variety of bead combinations, but you may have to change some of the caddis weave bead counts to accommodate different sizes of foundation beads. These instructions are for the white and gold bead shown above, right.

make the bead's foundation

Use the largest beads for the center row. As you work each row, choose beads that match closely in size and shape. Keep the tension tight as you work. Despite this, the foundation bead may be floppy until you add the caddis weave pass.

❶ Thread a needle with 2 yd. (1.8m) of conditioned Nymo. String two 6mm beads to the center of the thread and go through both beads again in the same direction. Align the beads so they sit side by side. String another bead and go through bead #2 from top to bottom. Come back up the third bead (**figure 1**).

String bead #4. Go through #3 from bottom to top and #4 again from top to bottom. Adding odd-numbered beads like #4 and even-numbered beads like #3, make a ladder of six 6mm beads (**figure 2**).

❷ To join the ends of the circle, pass the needle up through the first bead strung (**photo a**). Go down through the last bead and up through the first bead again.

❸ String two 6º seeds to begin the next row. Go under the thread bridge between the first and second beads and go back up through the last bead strung (**photo b**).

❹ String another 6º and go under the bridge between the next two beads (see brick stitch instructions on p. 7). Go back up through the new bead. Repeat with three more 6º beads.

❺ After stringing the sixth bead, go down through the first 6º. Then go up through the last 6º to complete the circular row.

❻ Repeat steps 3-5 to make a new row (six beads per row) with each of the following: rice pearls (**photo c**), 8ºs